Calorie Command:
A Practical Guide to Nutrition & Weight Loss

Coach Nick Schofield

Copyright © *Nicholas Schofield,* 2024
All Rights Reserved

This book is subject to the condition that no part of this book is to be reproduced, transmitted in any form or means; electronic or mechanical, stored in a retrieval system, photocopied, recorded, scanned, or otherwise. Any of these actions require the proper written permission of the author.

Dedication

I want to dedicate this book to my mother who I lost recently. She believed in all her children and supported us in our ventures. She was our rock.

Contents

Dedication i
Contents ii
Acknowledgments iii
Introduction iv
Disclaimer v
What are Macronutrients? 01
Calorie Counting for Weight Loss 5
Hydration 14
Nutrition for Optimal Human Performance 18
Other Considerations 22
Meal Ideas 26
Breakfast 27
Lunch 36
Evening Meal 46
Snacks 58
References 66
About the Author 68

Acknowledgments

I would like to thank my family for being patient and understanding over the last few years, as I juggled many projects with little spare time to enjoy family time. I could not have done half of what I achieved without your support.

Introduction

I have been asked why a nutrition book? As a former military member and current health and fitness coach, I often receive the same question: "What foods should I eat to increase my protein intake?" I understand that it can be challenging to find healthy, high-protein meals and snacks. That's why I've put together this book, which offers various breakfast, lunch, dinner, and snack options. These recipes are simple to prepare and will help you achieve your protein goals.

It is essential to keep in mind that these recipes are just suggestions and should be tailored to your specific needs and daily calorie intake. For best results, particularly if weight loss is you goal, incorporate these meals into an active lifestyle that includes both aerobic and resistance training.

In the early chapters, you'll find information about the fundamentals of nutrition and hydration to help you get started on your journey towards a healthy lifestyle.

Disclaimer

If you have any allergies, please check the ingredients to ensure you do not experience any adverse reactions. Some meals may contain nuts, fish, shellfish and dairy. Having said that, I do not have control over the ingredients you use to make these recipes nor the environment in which you make them, please be careful.

1. What are Macronutrients?

During my military career, nutrition was always an interest of mine, and this continued during my undergraduate degree where I completed a nutrition module to understand foods that improve performance. During basic training, I was very slim and struggled to build muscle. The gentleman at the Army Recruitment Centre told me to "drink Guinness and eat pies". Luckily times have changed, and the military have invested time into science to improve human performance. I started my military career at a stature of seven and a half stone (47 kg)! Although I could run like the wind, load carriage for me was very difficult. Carrying loads that met my body weight, made it very hard to focus on the task at hand. After basic training I decided to change this and started resistance training and trying to eat so much more. The changes were gradual but eventually I reached ten stone (63 kg) and went on to pass Pre-Parachute Selection and served with Airborne Forces. Diet, exercise and being consistent was key for this success. Remember progress is never linear, we have ups and down, we go backwards and then have great progress. Life deals us unexpected problems, and we must focus on these often sacrificing our own health and well-being. But the key is once this problem has been resolved, we get back to improving and continuing to look after ourselves. If you are consistent these periods will not have a huge impact on your progress. You will find that word a lot during this book, "consistent". Being consistent will pay dividends to your success.

Macronutrients are the fundamental components of our diet that provide energy and serve as the building blocks for bodily functions. Comprising carbohydrates, proteins, and fats, these nutrients play distinct roles in sustaining our overall health and well-being.

Carbohydrates

Carbohydrates are the primary source of energy for the body. They exist in various forms: simple carbohydrates found in sugars (like glucose and fructose) and complex carbohydrates present in foods like grains, vegetables, and legumes. The body breaks down carbs into glucose, which fuels our cells, muscles, and brain. However, not all carbohydrates are equal; some offer more nutritional value and fibre while others, like refined sugars, provide quick energy but lack essential nutrients.

Proteins

Proteins are crucial for building and repairing tissues, producing enzymes and hormones, and maintaining muscle mass. They are composed of amino acids, which the body uses to carry out various biological processes. Consuming a variety of protein sources—such as lean meats, fish, dairy, legumes, nuts, and seeds—ensures that your body receives all the essential amino acids necessary for optimal health.

Fats

Fats often get a bad reputation, but they are vital for our bodies. They act as a concentrated energy source, aid in the absorption of certain vitamins, and contribute to cell structure. Unsaturated fats (found in avocados, nuts, and olive oil) are considered healthier options compared to saturated fats (found in animal products) and trans fats (found in processed foods). Balancing fat intake is key for maintaining healthy cholesterol levels and supporting overall well-being.

Macronutrients During Exercise

When considering macronutrients for exercise, different macronutrients offer different benefits.

Carbohydrates

Energy Source: Carbohydrates are the body's primary and most readily available source of energy, especially during high-intensity and endurance exercises. This is due to its molecular structure having six oxygen atoms which supports aerobic energy production when conducting high intensity exercise.

Glycogen Stores: Carbohydrates are stored in muscles and the liver as glycogen, which serves as a fuel reserve. During exercise, these glycogen stores are utilised to sustain energy levels. Carbohydrates or its simplest form glycogen, is stored in the body with water. So, for every gram of glycogen stored, the body also stores around 3 – 4 grams of water. Now you can imagine how much extra weight that can increase but please do not worry this is normal. Why am I highlighting this? Well, in the past I have seen people be told to go on a low carbohydrate diet to lose weight. With the previous information it would make sense that as we deplete the amount of carbohydrates in the body, the more water we lose and the more weight we lose. Have we lost any fat? Maybe, but I would suggest that the weight is mainly water, and you can bet that this will increase once the individual starts to eat normally again, introducing carbohydrates. For exercise performance, you will realise carbohydrates are key to performing at a high level.

Timing: Consuming carbohydrates before workouts helps provide immediate energy, while consuming them after exercise aids in replenishing glycogen stores and facilitating muscle recovery. It is suggested that for intense or prolonged workouts, a meal high in complex carbohydrates two to four hours prior to the event is best. On the other hand, if you are close to the event starting (30-60 minutes) is it best to ingest a meal with simple carbohydrates, that will rapidly break down and digested providing a rapid energy boost. Simple carbohydrates in this scenario are things like fruit, cereal bar, or jam on toast. Unlike protein, carbohydrate uptake is maximised in the first two hours after exercise, it is also suggested that the increase in carbohydrates support anabolic state providing energy and allowing protein to repair and grow the body after being in a catabolic state.

Proteins

Muscle Repair and Growth: Proteins are crucial for repairing and building muscle tissues, which is essential for recovery and adaptation to exercise.

Amino Acids: The amino acids derived from protein intake are the building blocks of muscle tissue. Consuming protein post-exercise helps in muscle repair and growth. Muscle protein synthesis (MPS) is a continuous process but significantly increases after resistance exercise. This elevated state can last for around 24 to 48 hours. This obviously contradicts the widely thought process of an anabolic window being one hour after exercise. That said, the muscles are receptive to nutrients over this period, so if your daily protein is met, there is no need to be drinking protein shakes as you walk out of the gym.

Satiety and Muscle Maintenance: Adequate protein intake helps maintain muscle mass, supports satiety (feeling full), and aids in weight management during exercise routines.

Fats

Endurance Fuel: While fats are a slower source of energy compared to carbohydrates, they become essential during prolonged, low to moderate-intensity exercises like long-distance running or cycling.

Stored Energy: Fats stored in the body are utilised during low-intensity activities and serve as an energy reserve.

Vitamin Absorption: Some vitamins (A, D, E, and K) are fat-soluble, meaning they need fat to be absorbed by the body. Adequate fat intake supports overall health and performance.

Macronutrients are the cornerstone of a well-rounded diet. By understanding their roles and including a variety of sources in your meals, you can ensure that your body receives the necessary nutrients to function optimally. Remember, balance and moderation are key when it comes to consuming carbohydrates, proteins, and fats. Understanding how macronutrients function in relation to exercise helps athletes and fitness enthusiasts optimise their diet to support performance, endurance, recovery, and overall health. Balancing the intake of carbohydrates, proteins, and fats is crucial to meet the demands of different types of physical activities and achieve fitness goals.

2. Calorie Counting for Weight Loss

There are several diets that are common practice these days. Paleo, Atkins, Intermittent Fasting, Ketogenic and Vegan are a few diets used by the general population. The main aim of the diets is to reduce the number of calories ingested by individuals. Many people portray certain diets to have magical effects on fat utilisation and reduction. However, the science indicates that a calorie deficit is key, and I would add that sustainability is also key. What I am not going to do is shame these diets, but if you find one diet easier than others and it allows you to sustain it, then this is a great option for you. For example, a lot of people find intermittent fasting easier because you just miss out a meal, hence reducing calories. If this works, then great, use it to support your goals.

Over my career and time in the health and fitness industry, as a population we have demonised certain macronutrients. We blame one nutrient for poor health and increased weight when this is not the case. For example, in the earlier 1980's we demonised fat, then we started to understand the differences in fats. This changed the science and thoughts on high fat diets. It is more about the type of fats rather than the fat itself. Recently, we have seen carbohydrates get a bad reputation. Again, it is more on the type of carbohydrate rather than the carbohydrate itself. Simple carbohydrates do not give sustained energy, but they do have their uses which will be explained. No one nutrient will make you gain weight, over consuming calories will. However, getting all your calories from just fats, or just carbohydrates or just proteins, probably isn't the healthiest choice. Having a balanced diet is key with a mixture of all three nutrients, alongside colourful vegetables will improve your health and well-being.

Being plant based is a term being used recently and these terms can be misleading. It does not mean we just eat plants; it means most of your diet should be from plant-based sources. For example, a protein source such as fish, chicken, supported with a salad or vegetables such as peas, bean, potatoes cabbage etc.

There are several factors to consider when deciding on calorie counting for weight loss. Firstly, you must be in a calorie deficit, secondly it must be sustainable. Here are some tips to keep you focused on your weight loss journey:

- **Food Labels:** Utilise nutritional labels on packaged foods to understand calorie content per serving.

- **Portion Sizes:** Use measuring cups, food scales, or mobile apps to measure portions accurately.

- **Calorie-Tracking Apps**: There are various apps available that allow you to track your food intake and calculate calories consumed.

A word of warning, being in a calorie deficit seems a simple process and many coaches will say "calorie deficit" is the way. I do not deny this fact but when you consider the number of inaccuracies with the methods of tracking the deficit, it may seem more difficult that we first thought. For example, we can all remember the time when we weighed ourselves on different scales and seeing the weight change from one scale to another. I would suggest this being the same for food scales, there may be small differences in measurements. If you are using cups or tubs to measure your ingredients, again the amount may be slightly different each time. Imagine two pieces of chicken in a pack and the serving (100grams) says 31 grams of protein, the pack total weight is 300 grams. Now I acknowledge that they will do their best to measure the chicken pieces accurately, but I would suggest there could be some variation with this. These weights are regulated and there are some small tolerances but if you add this variation with your own measurement variation etc, then the inaccuracies can build up and can either be below your calorie deficit or above. We must also consider sauces, butter and oils added to food, this will also create inaccuracies in our calorie tracking.

So, what do I suggest? Aim for a calorie deficit and track changes over a two-week period. Metrics such as weight, clothes sizes and picture will allow you to gain a full idea of any changes. If you feel tired with limited energy, you may have dropped your calories too much. Remember is needs to be sustainable.

As always, everyone is different and some will be able to sustain bigger calorie deficits than others. As a rule of thumb the majority of people can sustain a calorie deficit of 500 calories day which is safe. This is generally broken down as 250 calories from diet and 250 calories from exercise. From experience I use a moderate deficit for someone first and then manipulate once they have managed to keep to this for a week or two weeks. It is advised to make small changes first to make them manageable, drastic changes can create issues and make it difficult to sustain.

When in a calorific deficit, ensuring that protein is high is key. This will help to maintain muscle tissue, hence the reason for this book! As a rule of thumb, it is suggested that a minimum of 1.2 g of protein per kg of weight daily to preserve muscle tissue. This number should be shared between each meal consumed. Numbers can increase up to 2 g of protein per kg of weight.

To be successful in calorie counting you must monitor and track your calories consistently. There are several methods and tools to help you do this. From experience most people prefer the mobile phone application that allows the phone to scan barcodes and uploads the calories according to the serving size. Just be mindful and ensure the serving size is correct. Plateaus are expected and may be experienced as the body adjusts, and in some cases adjusting the deficit or changing your exercise modalities can help overcome these plateaus.

While calorie counting is a useful tool, focusing solely on calories can overlook the nutritional quality of food. Prioritise nutrient-dense, whole foods over processed ones to ensure you are getting essential vitamins, minerals, and macronutrients. Try to prepare your meals daily as sometimes life can get in the way and time may be limited, this is when poor choices are made, and ultra-processed food are consumed.

Ultra- Processed Foods

Ultra-processed foods refer to food products that undergo extensive industrial processing, often containing additives, preservatives, and artificial substances. These foods are typically manufactured using several ingredients and additives, resulting in a product that's far removed from its original natural state. Here are some defining characteristics of ultra-processed foods:

- **Multiple Ingredients:** They contain numerous ingredients, including additives, sweeteners, stabilisers, colourants, and flavourings. These ingredients are often not found in typical kitchen settings.

- **Highly Industrialised:** They undergo multiple processes such as extrusion, hydrogenation, and high-temperature processing, altering their original structure and composition.

- **Low Nutritional Quality:** They tend to be low in essential nutrients like vitamins, minerals, and fiber while being high in unhealthy components such as added sugars, unhealthy fats, and sodium.

- **Convenience and Long Shelf Life:** These foods are designed for convenience, with a long shelf life making them easily accessible and suitable for long-term storage.

- **Ready-to-Consume:** Ultra-processed foods are often ready-to-consume or require minimal preparation, appealing to consumers looking for quick meals.

Examples of Ultra-Processed Foods:

- Sugary drinks (fizzy drinks, fruit-flavoured beverages)
- Processed meats (hot dogs, chicken nuggets)
- Instant noodles and soups
- Packaged snacks (chips, sweets)

- Breakfast cereals with added sugars
- Microwaveable frozen meals
- Industrialised bread and baked goods

Calorie counting is an effective method for weight management, providing insight into energy intake and expenditure. However, it's crucial to combine this approach with a balanced diet, regular exercise, and an understanding of overall nutritional needs for sustained weight loss and improved health. Reducing the consumption of ultra-processed foods and favouring whole, minimally processed foods like fruits, vegetables, whole grains, lean proteins, and healthy fats can significantly contribute to better overall health, weight management, and disease prevention.

A simple way to estimate your daily calorie intake is by using the Harris-Benedict equation or the Mifflin-St Jeor equation. These formulas estimate your Basal Metabolic Rate (BMR), which is the number of calories your body needs at rest to maintain basic physiological functions like breathing and circulation. Once you have your BMR, you can factor in your activity level using an activity multiplier to get an estimate of your total daily calorie needs.

Here's a basic breakdown:

- **Calculate your BMR** using one of these formulas:
    - For men: BMR = 88.362 + (13.397 × weight in kg) + (4.799 × height in cm) - (5.677 × age in years)
    - For women: BMR = 447.593 + (9.247 × weight in kg) + (3.098 × height in cm) - (4.330 × age in years)
- **Apply an activity multiplier** to your BMR based on your daily activity level:
    - Sedentary (little to no exercise): BMR × 1.2
    - Lightly active (light exercise/sports 1-3 days/week): BMR × 1.375

- Moderately active (moderate exercise/sports 3-5 days/week): BMR × 1.55
- Very active (hard exercise/sports 6-7 days/week): BMR × 1.725
- Extra active (very hard exercise/sports and physical job): BMR × 1.9

Example - 30-year-old, 75kg man who is 168cm in height and lightly active.

BMR= 88.362 + (13.397 x 75kg) + (4.799 x 168cm) - (5.677x 30)

BMR = 88.362 + (1004.76) + (806.23) - (170.31)

BMR= 1729.05

BMR + activity multiplier = 1729.05 x 1.375 (lightly active)

BMR= 2377daily calories, reduce calories as discussed (250kcal)

- **Adjust based on goals:** To lose weight, create a calorie deficit by consuming fewer calories than your estimated total daily energy expenditure. To gain weight, create a calorie surplus by consuming more calories than your estimated expenditure.

This method provides an estimate and might require adjustments based on individual factors like metabolism, body composition, and other lifestyle aspects. Consulting with a healthcare professional or nutritionist can offer personalized guidance for your specific needs.

So as a reminder, the key things to calorie counting:

- Choose a deficit that is sustainable, small gradual changes.
- Keep protein high to maintain muscle tissue.
- Measure foods, track calories and habits.
- Plan and prepare foods for each day.

- Stay away from ultra-processed foods.

- Keep consistent, so if you have a bad day, it won't have much of a dramatic effect on your progress.

My final tip do not be so hard on yourself. I have coached many people who rigidly control their calories. Life is for living and social events are normal. Having a break from counting calories will not make a difference in the grand scheme of things. It is about being consistent. However, if you are worried about overindulging during a social event, you can reduce your calories during the week, allowing you to relax more at the weekend.

3. Hydration

Hydration is key for human performance and to sustain life. During my time in the military, keeping hydrated during operations in a hot climate was very difficult. Carrying weighted backpacks in searing heat drained bodily fluids. During contacts with the enemy, keeping hydrated was the least of our problems. Some contacts could last for over two hours and believe me moving around between different cover is very exhausting. After we had returned to our camp, rehydration was key to the next patrol, or your performance was going to degrade hugely. From my experience in the health and wellbeing sector, I have seen peoples water intake improve. However, I conduct presentations on workforce health and wellbeing in different industries, and this is not the case outside the health and wellbeing industry. Most active workforces, especially nightshift workers live on caffeine. This beverage is a diuretic and will increase fluid expenditure increasing the chances of dehydration. With our nations love for coffee, I would suggest drinking a glass of water for each cup of caffeinated beverage you have.

Water is the said to be the source of life, it is involved in many chemical reactions in the body, especially the breakdown and building of the major components of the cell. Water is fundamental to human survival. Our bodies are composed of approximately 60% water, and it is involved in almost every bodily function, from regulating body temperature to aiding in digestion and nutrient absorption. Water serves as a carrier, transporting essential nutrients, vitamins, and minerals to cells throughout the body. It is crucial for the proper circulation of blood, ensuring oxygen and nutrients reach all tissues and organs.

The benefits of adequate hydration are:

1. Enhanced Physical Performance

Proper hydration is integral to optimal physical performance. It aids in regulating body temperature, lubricating joints, and delivering nutrients and oxygen to cells. Athletes and active individuals often notice improved endurance and reduced fatigue when adequately hydrated.

2. Cognitive Function and Mental Clarity

The brain requires adequate hydration to function optimally. Dehydration can impair cognitive function, leading to decreased focus, mood swings, and difficulty in concentration. Staying hydrated supports mental clarity, alertness, and overall cognitive performance.

3. Regulation of Body Functions

Hydration plays a key role in various bodily functions. It helps maintain blood pressure, supports proper digestion, facilitates nutrient absorption, and aids in the removal of waste and toxins through urine.

4. Joint and Muscle Health

Proper hydration ensures that joints remain lubricated, and muscles are adequately supplied with fluids, reducing the risk of cramps, and supporting overall joint health during physical activities.

5. Skin Health and Appearance

Adequate hydration contributes to healthy, glowing skin. It helps maintain skin elasticity, preventing dryness, and can reduce the signs of premature aging.

Implications of Dehydration

1. Decreased Physical Performance

Even mild dehydration can lead to reduced physical performance, impacting endurance, strength, and coordination. It can cause early fatigue, muscle cramps, and heat-related illnesses during exercise or high-temperature environments.

2. Cognitive Impairment

Dehydration affects cognitive function, leading to reduced alertness, impaired concentration, and memory issues. Prolonged dehydration can even result in confusion and disorientation.

3. Negative Impact on Health

Chronic dehydration can have long-term health implications. It's associated with an increased risk of kidney stones, urinary tract infections, and in severe cases, it may contribute to kidney damage or failure.

4. Heat-Related Illnesses

In hot climates or during intense physical activity, inadequate hydration can lead to heat exhaustion or heatstroke. These conditions are serious and require immediate medical attention.

5. Skin and Digestive Issues

Dehydration can result in dry, flaky skin and worsen conditions like eczema. Additionally, insufficient hydration may lead to digestive problems such as constipation due to lack of water to soften stool.

Maintaining Proper Hydration

1. Water Intake

Regularly consume water throughout the day. Individual water needs vary based on factors like climate, physical activity, and overall health, but a general guideline is around 2-3 litres (8-12 cups) daily.

2. Electrolyte Balance

In situations involving excessive sweating (during intense exercise or in hot environments), replenishing electrolytes along with fluids is crucial to maintain proper hydration levels.

3. Monitor Urine Colour

Monitoring urine colour can be a simple way to gauge hydration status. Clear to light yellow urine generally indicates adequate hydration, while dark yellow or amber-coloured urine may signal dehydration.

4. Dietary Sources of Hydration

Include hydrating foods like fruits (watermelon, oranges), vegetables (cucumbers, tomatoes), and soups in your diet to contribute to overall hydration.

Maintaining proper hydration is paramount for overall health and well-being. From supporting physical performance and cognitive function to regulating bodily functions, adequate hydration is foundational for optimal health. Be mindful of your water intake and stay hydrated to enjoy the multitude of benefits it offers.

4. Nutrition for Optimal Human Performance

Nutrition plays a pivotal role in the performance, recovery, and overall health of athletes, particularly tactical athletes who require a blend of strength, endurance, and mental acuity. This chapter delves into the science of fuelling for different types of training sessions, with a specific focus on resistance and endurance training. I have discussed the importance of carbohydrates and protein early in this book but in this chapter I will focus more on these macronutrients for performance in an exercise setting. We will also discuss post-exercise refueling, to optimize recovery.

Fuelling for Resistance Training

Pre-Workout Nutrition:

Carbohydrates: As discussed earlier, carbohydrates are the primary energy source during resistance training. Consuming a meal rich in complex carbohydrates 2-3 hours before a workout helps to maintain glycogen stores. Examples include whole grains, fruits, and vegetables.

Protein: Ingesting protein before exercise supports muscle protein synthesis and helps prevent muscle breakdown. Aim for 20-30 grams of high-quality protein, such as chicken, fish, eggs, or a protein shake, 1-2 hours before training.

Hydration: Adequate hydration is essential for muscle function and overall performance. Drink 500-600 ml of water in the hours leading up to your session.

During Workout:

For most resistance training sessions lasting less than 60 minutes, water is sufficient. For longer sessions, a sports drink containing electrolytes and carbohydrates may be beneficial to sustain energy levels.

Post-Workout Nutrition:

Protein: Post-workout protein intake is crucial for muscle repair and growth. Aim for 20-40 grams of high-quality protein after your session. The "anabolic window" of 30-60 minutes does not seem to be supported these days. Muscle protein synthesis is elevated for at least 24 hours, so consuming the normal daily protein amounts is suggested to be optimal. As a reminder this ranges from 1.5 grams to 2 grams of protein for every kg of body weight. Whey protein shakes, lean meats, and dairy products are excellent choices.

Carbohydrates: To replenish glycogen stores, consume 1-1.2 grams of carbohydrates per kilogram of body weight immediately after your workout. This can be achieved through fruits, whole grains, or carbohydrate-based recovery drinks.

Hydration: Rehydration is vital to replace fluids lost through sweat. Include electrolytes in your recovery drink if you had an intense workout.

Fuelling for Endurance Training

Pre-Workout Nutrition:

Carbohydrates: A high-carbohydrate meal 3-4 hours before your endurance session helps to maximise glycogen stores. Include foods such as pasta, rice, oats, and fruits.

Protein: Including a moderate amount of protein (10-20 grams) can help sustain energy and aid in muscle repair during long sessions.

Hydration: Begin your workout well-hydrated by drinking 500-600 ml of water or an electrolyte solution in the hours leading up to your session.

During Workout:

Carbohydrates: For sessions lasting longer than 60 minutes, consume 30-60 grams of carbohydrates per hour. This can be achieved through sports drinks, energy gels, or easily digestible snacks like bananas or energy bars.

Hydration: Drink small amounts of water regularly to maintain hydration. For longer sessions, use electrolyte solutions to prevent dehydration and electrolyte imbalances.

Post-Workout Nutrition:

Carbohydrates: Rapidly replenish glycogen stores by consuming 1-1.5 grams of carbohydrates per kilogram of body weight within 30 minutes of finishing your workout. It is suggested that simple carbohydrates are best during this period. They are rapidly digested and absorbed.

Protein: Include 20-30 grams of protein to aid muscle recovery and repair. This can come from lean meats, dairy, eggs, or protein supplements.

Hydration: Rehydrate with water or an electrolyte solution to replace fluids lost through sweat.

Special Considerations for Tactical Athletes

Although I coach different types of populations, I tend to focus on the Tactical Athlete cohort. All previous sections can be pertinent to anyone wishing to have a healthy balanced diet. However, when it comes to performance, in particular the Tactical Athlete population, there are a few nuisances that need to be discussed. Tactical Athletes, due to their physical role, need to be more focused to ensure they replenish macronutrients and support recovery after each action, to ensure optimal performance at all times.

Balanced Diet: Tactical athletes should consume a balanced diet rich in fruits, vegetables, lean proteins, whole grains, and healthy fats to ensure they receive all essential nutrients.

Nutrient Timing: Strategic nutrient timing around training sessions is crucial for maintaining energy levels and promoting recovery. This includes consuming carbohydrates and proteins both pre- and post-workout. If two sessions are planned within a 24 hour period, carbohydrates become more crucial to ensure energy balance and support performance in the second session of this period. This will also aid in muscle protein synthesis. Without delving too deep in molecular physiology, if energy balances are low, the body can stop muscle protein synthesis to reduce energy consumption. The bottom line being, consume carbohydrates after each session to replenish glycogen stores and improve recovery.

Remember, when on exercise, or operations, Tactical Athletes may need to deploy at a moments notice. Having consumed the right macronutrients post patrol or operation action, will support your performance later when required.

Supplements: While whole foods should be the primary source of nutrients, certain supplements such as omega-3 fatty acids, vitamin D, and B vitamins can support overall health and performance. Consult with a healthcare provider before starting any supplement regimen.

Visual Guide: Pre-Workout Meal Example

- Porridge topped with banana slices and a spoonful of honey.
- Grilled chicken breast with quinoa and mixed vegetables.
- A smoothie made with Greek yoghurt, berries, and a handful of spinach.

Optimising nutrition for resistance and endurance training involves strategic planning and an understanding of the body's needs before, during, and after exercise. For tactical athletes, this approach ensures they are not only physically prepared but also mentally sharp and resilient. By following these guidelines, athletes can enhance their performance, speed up recovery, and maintain overall health.

5. Other Considerations

Thermal Effects of Food

The thermal effect of food (TEF) is the energy required by the body to process and metabolise the food consumed. Understanding TEF can aid in managing weight and improving metabolic health. Foods high in protein have a higher thermal effect compared to carbohydrates and fats, meaning they require more energy to break down and absorb.

Proteins increase the body's metabolic rate more significantly than other macronutrients, making high-protein foods beneficial for weight management and muscle maintenance. This is because proteins are essential for repairing tissues and supporting immune function, and their higher TEF contributes to increased calorie burning. Including a variety of protein sources such as lean meats, dairy, legumes, and plant-based proteins can help optimise metabolic health and support weight loss efforts.

Cooking methods significantly influence the thermal effect of food. Cooked foods are generally easier to digest than raw foods, reducing the overall energy expenditure. However, certain cooking methods like steaming or boiling can preserve more nutrients compared to frying or baking at high temperatures. Understanding how different cooking methods affect the energy your body expends during digestion can help optimize your diet for better energy management and nutrient retention.

Additionally, the thermal effect varies among different food types. For instance, fibrous vegetables and whole grains require more energy to break down, contributing to a higher TEF. Incorporating a balanced mix of macronutrients and choosing foods that are more thermogenic can enhance the diet's effectiveness in supporting metabolic health and weight management.

Balancing the diet with a mix of macronutrients and selecting appropriate cooking methods can optimise the thermal effects of food, supporting overall metabolic health. This knowledge is particularly useful for individuals looking to enhance their diet's effectiveness in weight management and overall wellness, ensuring a well-rounded approach to nutrition and health.

Health and Wellbeing and How It Can Be Supported with Nutrition

Nutrition plays a pivotal role in maintaining and enhancing overall health and wellbeing. A balanced diet, rich in essential nutrients, supports physical, mental, and emotional health. Consuming a variety of foods from all food groups ensures that the body receives a comprehensive range of vitamins, minerals, and macronutrients necessary for optimal functioning.

A balanced diet impacts physical health by supporting the functioning of vital organs, strengthening the immune system, and contributing to muscle and bone health. Foods high in antioxidants, such as berries, leafy greens, and nuts, can help reduce inflammation and protect against chronic diseases. Adequate intake of calcium and vitamin D is crucial for maintaining strong bones, while iron-rich foods like red meat and legumes are vital for blood health. Additionally, a well-balanced diet aids in maintaining healthy skin, hair, and nails, reflecting overall health.

Mental health is profoundly affected by dietary choices. Certain nutrients, particularly omega-3 fatty acids found in oily fish, and B vitamins in whole grains, play a significant role in brain health. These nutrients can improve mood, cognitive function, and reduce the risk of disorders such as depression and anxiety. A diet rich in these nutrients can lead to enhanced memory, sharper focus, and more stable emotions.

Emotional wellbeing is also influenced by nutrition. Eating regular, balanced meals helps regulate blood sugar levels, which in turn can stabilize mood swings and energy levels throughout the day. Mindful eating practices encourage a healthier relationship with food and body image. Listening to your body's hunger and fullness cues is essential to foster a positive eating environment and avoid emotional eating patterns.

Incorporating a variety of nutrient-dense foods, staying hydrated, and adjusting dietary choices to individual needs are key strategies to support health and wellbeing through nutrition. Engaging in regular physical activity complements a nutritious diet and amplifies the benefits on overall health. By understanding the link between diet and wellbeing, individuals can make informed choices that enhance their quality of life and long-term health outcomes.

Seasonal and Cultural Adaptations in Nutrition

Adapting nutritional practices according to seasonal availability and cultural preferences can enhance the enjoyment and health benefits of meals. Eating seasonally ensures that fruits and vegetables are at their peak in flavour and nutritional value, while embracing cultural adaptations can introduce a broader spectrum of nutrients and culinary experiences.

Seasonal eating involves focusing on fresh fruits and vegetables like berries, leafy greens, and tomatoes in spring and summer. These foods are not only lighter and more refreshing but also provide essential vitamins and hydration during warmer months. In autumn and winter, root vegetables and hearty grains like squash, potatoes, and whole grains are excellent for sustaining energy and providing warmth during colder weather. Seasonal eating supports local agriculture, often resulting in fresher, more flavourful meals, and reduces the environmental impact of food transport.

Cultural variations in diet reflect each culture's unique dietary staples and cooking methods. For example, Mediterranean diets, rich in olive oil, fish, and nuts, promote heart health, while traditional Japanese diets, which include fermented foods and seafood, support digestive health and longevity. Exploring these diverse diets can offer insights into new flavours and ways to incorporate a range of nutrients beneficial for health.

Incorporating seasonal and culturally diverse foods into the diet can make meals more interesting and nutritionally balanced. This approach supports sustainable eating practices by favouring local and seasonal produce and introduces a variety of tastes and textures that can cater to different dietary preferences and nutritional needs. By understanding and embracing these adaptations, individuals can enjoy a richer, more diverse dietary experience that contributes to overall health and wellbeing.

6. Meal Ideas

The recipes I have chosen are high in protein and quick to make and relatively cheap. With the current situation with the cost of living, it is key that each nutritious meal is inexpensive. Good food does not have to be expensive.

I have broken down each meal section into breakfast, lunch, evening meal and finally snacks. I have used simple directions to guide you through the meal preparation process. Each meal is broken down into total macronutrients. I have tried to keep the preparation time to under 20 minutes, but some may be over. We all have a busy daily life and having a large preparation time is only going to reduce time available for other things, such as family time.

Note: Breakfast, lunch, and snacks are single serving meals, dinner is for a family of four.

7. Breakfast

Protein- Packed Breakfast Burrito

Ingredients:

- 2 large eggs
- 30g shredded cheese
- 1 whole-wheat tortilla
- Salsa or diced tomatoes (optional)
- Salt, pepper, and spices to taste

Macronutrient Breakdown (per serving):

- Protein: 25g
- Fat: 15g
- Carbs: 30g

Instructions:

- Scramble eggs in a pan, and cook until heated.
- Sprinkle shredded cheese over the mixture and allow it to melt.
- Spoon the mixture onto a warmed tortilla, add salsa or diced tomatoes if desired, fold, and enjoy!

Greek Yogurt Protein Bowl

Ingredients:

- 200g Greek yogurt
- 30g granola
- 20g mixed nuts
- 50g mixed berries
- Honey or agave syrup (optional)

Macronutrient Breakdown (per serving):

- Protein: 20g
- Fat: 15g
- Carbs: 40g

Instructions:

- Spoon Greek yogurt into a bowl.
- Top with granola, mixed nuts, and mixed berries.
- Drizzle honey or agave syrup for added sweetness if desired. Mix and enjoy!

Spinach and Feta Breakfast Quesadilla

Ingredients:

- 2 large eggs
- 50g fresh spinach
- 30g crumbled feta cheese
- 1 whole-wheat tortilla
- Salt, pepper, and spices to taste

Macronutrient Breakdown (per serving):

- Protein: 20g
- Fat: 15g
- Carbs: 25g

Instructions:

- Scramble eggs in a pan, add fresh spinach, and cook until wilted.
- Sprinkle crumbled feta cheese over one half of the tortilla.
- Spoon the egg and spinach mixture over the cheese, fold the tortilla in half, and cook on both sides until golden brown.

Smoked Salmon and Scrambled Eggs on Wholegrain Toast

Ingredients:

- 2 large eggs
- 50g smoked salmon
- 2 slices of wholegrain bread
- 1 tsp butter
- Chives for garnish (optional)

Macronutrient Breakdown (per serving):

- Protein: 25g
- Fat: 15g
- Carbs: 20g

Instructions:

- Scramble eggs with a splash of milk in a pan over medium heat, stirring until cooked to your liking.
- Toast wholegrain bread and spread with butter.
- Place the scrambled eggs on the toast, top with smoked salmon, and garnish with chives if desired.

Full English Wrap

Ingredients:

- 2 large eggs
- 2 rashers of bacon
- 1 pork sausage
- 1 whole-wheat tortilla
- 30g baked beans
- Grilled tomato and mushrooms (optional)

Macronutrient Breakdown (per serving):

- Protein: 30g
- Fat: 25g
- Carbs: 25g

Instructions:

- Cook bacon, sausage, eggs, grilled tomato, and mushrooms in a pan until cooked through.
- Warm the tortilla and spread baked beans across the centre.
- Place cooked ingredients onto the tortilla, fold, and wrap to enjoy a protein-packed breakfast wrap.

Smoked Salmon and Cream Cheese Bagel

Ingredients:

- 1 whole-grain bagel
- 50g smoked salmon
- 30g cream cheese
- Fresh dill for garnish (optional)

Macronutrient Breakdown (per serving):

- Protein: 25g
- Fat: 15g
- Carbs: 35g

Instructions:

- Toast the whole-grain bagel until golden brown.
- Spread cream cheese evenly on both halves of the bagel.
- Top with smoked salmon and garnish with fresh dill if desired. Serve open-faced or as a sandwich.

High Protein Porridge with Berries and Nuts

Ingredients:

- 50g rolled oats
- 200ml milk
- 20g mixed nuts
- 50g mixed berries
- Honey or maple syrup (optional)
- Cinnamon or nutmeg (optional)

Macronutrient Breakdown (per serving):

- Protein: 15g
- Fat: 10g
- Carbs: 40g

Instructions:

- Cook rolled oats with milk until creamy.
- Serve in a bowl, top with mixed nuts, mixed berries, and a drizzle of honey or maple syrup.
- Sprinkle cinnamon or nutmeg for added flavour if desired and enjoy.

Poached Eggs on Toast with Avocado and Chilli Jam

Ingredients:

- 2 eggs
- 2 slices of whole-grain bread
- 1 ripe avocado
- 2 tbsp chili jam
- Salt and pepper to taste
- Fresh parsley for garnish (optional)

Macronutrient Breakdown (per serving):

- Protein: 14g
- Fat: 25g
- Carbs: 40g

Instructions:

- Prepare the Poached Eggs.
- Toast the Bread.
- Prepare the Avocado:
    - Halve the avocado, remove the pit, and scoop the flesh into a bowl.
    - Mash the avocado with a fork and season with salt and pepper to taste.
- Assemble.

8. Lunch

Tuna and Chickpea Salad

Ingredients:

- 100g canned tuna
- 50g chickpeas
- Mixed salad leaves
- 30g cherry tomatoes
- 1/4 cucumber
- 1 tbsp olive oil
- Lemon juice, salt, and pepper to taste

Macronutrient Breakdown (per serving):

- Protein: 20g
- Fat: 10g
- Carbs: 15g

Instructions:

- Drain the canned tuna and chickpeas.
- Chop the cucumber and cherry tomatoes.
- Mix the tuna, chickpeas, mixed salad leaves, cucumber, and tomatoes in a bowl.
- Drizzle with olive oil, lemon juice, and season with salt and pepper.

Chicken and Quinoa Bowl

Ingredients:

- 100g cooked chicken breast
- 50g cooked quinoa
- 50g mixed vegetables
- 1 tbsp Greek yogurt
- Fresh herbs for garnish (optional)
- Salt, pepper, and spices to taste

Macronutrient Breakdown (per serving):

- Protein: 25g
- Fat: 5g
- Carbs: 20g

Instructions:

- Cook chicken breast and quinoa separately.
- Steam or stir-fry mixed vegetables.
- Place cooked quinoa in a bowl, top with sliced chicken, mixed vegetables, and a dollop of Greek yogurt.
- Garnish with fresh herbs if desired.

Jacket Sweet Potato with Cottage Cheese

Ingredients:

- 1 medium sweet potato
- 100g cottage cheese
- 30g mixed seeds
- Mixed salad leaves
- Salt, pepper, and herbs to taste

Macronutrient Breakdown (per serving):

- Protein: 15g
- Fat: 10g
- Carbs: 30g

Instructions:

- Bake the sweet potato until soft.
- Slice open the sweet potato, top with cottage cheese, and sprinkle with mixed seeds.
- Serve with a side of mixed salad leaves, seasoned with salt, pepper, and herbs.

Lentil and Vegetable Soup

Ingredients:

- 100g dry lentils
- 1 onion, diced
- 2 carrots, chopped
- 2 celery stalks, chopped
- 1 can chopped tomatoes
- 1 litre vegetable broth
- 1 tbsp olive oil
- Herbs and spices to taste

Macronutrient Breakdown (per serving):

- Protein: 15g
- Fat: 5g
- Carbs: 30g

Instructions:

- Rinse lentils and set aside.
- In a pot, sauté onions, carrots, and celery in olive oil until softened.
- Add lentils, chopped tomatoes, vegetable broth, and season with herbs and spices.
- Simmer for 25-30 minutes until lentils are tender.

Chicken and Mushroom Risotto

Ingredients:

- 100g Arborio rice
- 150g cooked chicken breast, shredded
- 100g mushrooms, sliced
- 1 onion, finely chopped
- 1 litre chicken broth
- 2 tbsp grated Parmesan cheese
- Salt, pepper, and herbs to taste

Macronutrient Breakdown (per serving):

- Protein: 20g
- Fat: 5g
- Carbs: 30g

Instructions:

- In a pan, sauté onions until translucent.
- Add mushrooms and cook until they release their moisture.
- Stir in Arborio rice and cook until it's lightly toasted.
- Gradually add chicken broth, stirring continuously until the rice is cooked.
- Mix in shredded chicken, Parmesan cheese, and season with salt, pepper, and herbs.

Baked Salmon with Sweet Potato Mash

Ingredients:

- 150g salmon fillet
- 2 medium sweet potatoes
- 1 tbsp olive oil
- 1 lemon, sliced
- Salt, pepper, and herbs to taste

Macronutrient Breakdown (per serving):

- Protein: 25g
- Fat: 15g
- Carbs: 30g

Instructions:

- Preheat the oven to 200°C (392°F).
- Rub salmon with olive oil, season with salt, pepper, and herbs.
- Place salmon on a baking tray with lemon slices and bake for 15-20 minutes.
- Boil and mash sweet potatoes, season to taste.
- Serve the salmon over a bed of sweet potato mash.

Beef and Vegetable Stir-Fry

Ingredients:

- 150g lean beef strips
- 100g mixed vegetables
- 50g cooked brown rice
- 1 tbsp soy sauce
- 1 tbsp olive oil
- Salt, pepper, and spices to taste

Macronutrient Breakdown (per serving):

- Protein: 30g
- Fat: 12g
- Carbs: 25g

Instructions:

- Heat olive oil in a pan, add beef strips, and cook until browned.
- Add mixed vegetables and stir-fry until tender-crisp.
- Add cooked brown rice and soy sauce, season with salt, pepper, and spices, and stir-fry for another minute.

Lentil and Chicken Soup

Ingredients:

- 100g cooked chicken breast
- 50g lentils
- 1 carrot, chopped
- 1 celery stalk, chopped
- 500ml chicken or vegetable broth
- Fresh herbs for garnish (optional)
- Salt, pepper, and spices to taste

Macronutrient Breakdown (per serving):

- Protein: 25g
- Fat: 5g
- Carbs: 20g

Instructions:

- In a pot, bring the broth to a simmer and add lentils, carrot, and celery.
- Simmer for 15-20 minutes until lentils and vegetables are tender.
- Add cooked chicken, season with salt, pepper, and spices, and simmer for another 5 minutes.
- Garnish with fresh herbs before serving.

Baked Beans and Sausage Casserole

Ingredients:

- 2 sausages
- 200g canned baked beans
- 1 onion, diced
- 1 garlic clove, minced
- 1 tbsp olive oil
- Mixed herbs and spices
- 50g grated cheese for topping

Macronutrient Breakdown (per serving):

- Protein: 18g
- Fat: 15g
- Carbs: 30g

Instructions:

- Preheat oven to 180°C (350°F).
- In an ovenproof dish, heat olive oil, sauté onions and garlic until soft.
- Add sausages and cook until browned. Stir in baked beans and mixed herbs/spices.
- Top with grated cheese and bake for 20-25 minutes until bubbly and golden.

9. Evening Meal

Baked Lemon Herb Chicken with Roasted Vegetables

Ingredients:

- 1.5 kg chicken thighs
- 1 kg mixed vegetables (potatoes, carrots, bell peppers)
- Olive oil, lemon juice, herbs, salt, and pepper for seasoning

Macronutrient Breakdown (per serving; family of 4):

- Protein: 40g per serving
- Fat: 15g per serving
- Carbs: 20g per serving

Instructions:

- Preheat oven to 200°C (400°F).
- Season chicken thighs with olive oil, lemon juice, herbs, salt, and pepper.
- Place chicken on a baking tray, surround with chopped vegetables, and drizzle with olive oil.
- Bake for 40-45 mins or until chicken is cooked and vegetables are tender.

Lentil and Vegetable Stew with Crusty Bread

Ingredients:

- 500g lentils
- 1 kg mixed vegetables (onions, carrots, celery)
- 4 slices crusty bread
- Vegetable broth, olive oil, herbs, salt, and spices

Macronutrient Breakdown (per serving; family of 4):

- Protein: 20g per serving
- Fat: 5g per serving
- Carbs: 35g per serving

Instructions:

- Cook lentils in vegetable broth until tender.
- Sauté chopped onions, carrots, and celery in olive oil until softened.
- Combine cooked vegetables with lentils, season with herbs, salt, and spices.
- Serve the stew with crusty bread slices.

Spaghetti Bolognese with Lean Ground Turkey

Ingredients:

- 500g lean ground turkey
- 400g whole-grain spaghetti
- 1 can (400g) crushed tomatoes
- 1 onion, diced
- 2 cloves garlic, minced
- 2 carrots, grated
- Italian herbs, salt, and pepper to taste

Macronutrient Breakdown (per serving):

- Protein: 30g
- Fat: 5g
- Carbs: 50g

Instructions:

- Brown ground turkey in a large pan.
- Add diced onions, minced garlic, and grated carrots. Cook until softened.
- Pour in crushed tomatoes, season with Italian herbs, salt, and pepper. Simmer for 20-30 minutes.
- Cook spaghetti according to package instructions.
- Serve Bolognese sauce over cooked spaghetti.

Chicken and Vegetable Stir-Fry with Brown Rice

Ingredients:

- 500g chicken breast, sliced
- 400g mixed vegetables (broccoli, bell peppers, snap peas)
- 2 cups brown rice, cooked
- Soy sauce, ginger, garlic, and sesame oil for stir-fry
- Salt and pepper to taste

Macronutrient Breakdown (per serving):

- Protein: 35g
- Fat: 5g
- Carbs: 50g

Instructions:

- Stir-fry sliced chicken in a pan with soy sauce, ginger, garlic, and sesame oil until cooked.
- Add mixed vegetables and cook until they are crisp-tender.
- Season with salt and pepper.
- Serve over cooked brown rice.

One Pan Baked Thighs with Vegetables

Ingredients:

- 8 chicken thighs
- 500g mixed vegetables (carrots, broccoli, bell peppers)
- Olive oil, garlic, paprika, salt, and pepper for seasoning

Macronutrient Breakdown (per serving):

- Protein: 35g
- Fat: 15g
- Carbs: 15g

Instructions:

- Preheat the oven to 200°C (400°F).
- Place chicken thighs and chopped vegetables on a baking sheet.
- Drizzle with olive oil, season with minced garlic, paprika, salt, and pepper.
- Bake for 30-40 minutes or until the chicken is cooked through and vegetables are tender.

Turkey and Black Bean Tacos

Ingredients:

- 500g ground turkey
- 2 cans black beans
- Taco seasoning (cumin, paprika, chili powder)
- 1 onion, diced
- Taco shells or tortillas
- Toppings: lettuce, tomato, cheese, salsa (optional)

Macronutrient Breakdown (per serving):

- Protein: 20g
- Fat: 10g
- Carbs: 25g

Instructions:

- Cook diced onion in a pan until softened. Add ground turkey and cook until browned.
- Stir in taco seasoning and black beans (drained and rinsed). Cook until heated through.
- Warm taco shells or tortillas.
- Fill shells with the turkey and black bean mixture and add desired toppings.

Quinoa and Vegetable Stir-Fry with Tofu

Ingredients:

- 400g firm tofu
- 1 cup quinoa
- 1kg mixed stir-fry vegetables (such as broccoli, bell peppers, and snow peas)
- Soy sauce, garlic, ginger, olive oil
- Optional: sesame seeds for garnish

Macronutrient Breakdown (per serving):

- Protein: 18g
- Fat: 10g
- Carbs: 35g

Instructions:

- Cook quinoa according to package instructions.
- Press tofu to remove excess water, then cube it.
- Sauté tofu cubes in olive oil until golden. Remove from the pan.
- Stir-fry mixed vegetables with garlic and ginger. Add tofu back in.
- Toss with soy sauce and serve over cooked quinoa. Garnish with sesame seeds if desired.

Honey Garlic Glazed Chicken with Roasted Vegetables

Ingredients:

- 8 chicken thighs
- 1kg mixed vegetables (such as carrots, broccoli, and bell peppers)
- Honey, soy sauce, garlic, olive oil, salt, and pepper

Macronutrient Breakdown (per serving):

- Protein: 30g
- Fat: 15g
- Carbs: 20g

Instructions:

- Preheat oven to 200°C (400°F).
- Place chicken thighs on a baking sheet. Season with salt and pepper.
- Mix honey, soy sauce, minced garlic, and olive oil. Brush over chicken.
- Toss mixed vegetables with olive oil, salt, and pepper. Spread them around the chicken on the baking sheet.
- Roast for 25-30 minutes or until chicken is cooked through and vegetables are tender.

Beef and Vegetable Skewers

Ingredients:

- 600g beef chunks
- Assorted vegetables (bell peppers, onions, cherry tomatoes)
- 2 tablespoons olive oil
- Salt, pepper, paprika, garlic powder
- Skewers

Macronutrient Breakdown (per serving):

- Protein: 28g
- Fat: 15g
- Carbs: 10g

Instructions:

- Preheat grill or broiler.
- Thread beef chunks and assorted vegetables onto skewers.
- Brush skewers with olive oil and season with salt, pepper, paprika, and garlic powder.
- Grill or broil skewers for 10-15 minutes, turning occasionally until beef is cooked to desired doneness.
- Serve the skewers hot.

Beef and Vegetable Skillet with Quinoa

Ingredients:

- 500g beef sirloin strips
- 1 cup quinoa
- 1kg mixed vegetables (bell peppers, cherry tomatoes)
- 2 tablespoons balsamic vinegar
- 2 tablespoons olive oil
- Salt, pepper, dried herbs

Macronutrient Breakdown (per serving):

- Protein: 35g
- Fat: 15g
- Carbs: 35g

Instructions:

- Cook quinoa according to package instructions.
- In a skillet, heat olive oil and cook beef until browned.
- Add mixed vegetables and cook until they start to soften.
- Drizzle balsamic vinegar over the mixture and season with salt, pepper, and dried herbs.
- Serve the beef and vegetable skillet over cooked quinoa.

Salmon Pasta with Creamy Alfredo Sauce

Ingredients:

- 500g salmon fillet
- 500g pasta
- 1 cup heavy cream
- 1 cup grated Parmesan cheese
- 2 garlic cloves, minced
- Olive oil, salt, and pepper

Macronutrient Breakdown (per serving):

- Protein: 30g
- Fat: 20g
- Carbs: 45g

Instructions:

- Cook pasta according to package instructions.
- Season salmon with olive oil, salt, and pepper. Cook until flaky and set aside.
- In a pan, sauté minced garlic in olive oil. Add heavy cream and simmer.
- Stir in grated Parmesan cheese until the sauce thickens.
- Toss cooked pasta with the creamy Alfredo sauce and top with flaked salmon.

10. Snacks

Peanut Butter Energy Balls

Ingredients:

- 1 cup old-fashioned oats
- 1/2 cup peanut butter
- 1/4 cup honey
- 1/4 cup chocolate chips or chopped nuts (optional)
- 1 tablespoon chia seeds or flaxseeds

Macronutrient Breakdown (per serving - 2 energy balls):

- Protein: 8g
- Fat: 10g
- Carbs: 20g

Instructions:

- In a bowl, mix oats, peanut butter, honey or maple syrup, chocolate chips or nuts, and chia seeds or flaxseeds until well combined.
- Roll the mixture into bite-sized balls.
- Place in the refrigerator for 30 minutes to set. Store in an airtight container.

Cottage Cheese and Veggie Dip

Ingredients:

- 1 cup cottage cheese
- Assorted chopped vegetables (carrots, cucumber, bell peppers)
- Seasonings like black pepper, paprika, or mixed herbs

Macronutrient Breakdown (per serving - 1/2 cup dip with veggies):

- Protein: 15g
- Fat: 3g
- Carbs: 10g

Instructions:

- Blend or process the cottage cheese until smooth.
- Add desired seasonings and mix well.
- Serve with chopped vegetables for dipping.

Roasted Chickpeas

Ingredients:

- 2 cans chickpeas, drained and rinsed
- 2 tablespoons olive oil
- Seasonings (such as garlic powder, paprika, cumin, salt)

Macronutrient Breakdown (per serving - 1/2 cup roasted chickpeas):

- Protein: 7g
- Fat: 5g
- Carbs: 20g

Instructions:

- Preheat oven to 200°C (400°F).
- Pat dry the chickpeas and toss with olive oil and desired seasonings.
- Spread the chickpeas on a baking sheet in a single layer.
- Roast for 25-30 minutes until crispy, shaking the pan occasionally.
- Let them cool before enjoying as a crunchy snack.

Peanut Butter and Banana Rice Cakes

Ingredients:

- 4 rice cakes
- 4 tablespoons peanut butter
- 2 bananas, sliced

Macronutrient Breakdown (per serving):

- Protein: 10g
- Fat: 12g
- Carbs: 30g

Instructions:

- Spread peanut butter evenly over each rice cake.
- Top with banana slices.
- Enjoy these delicious and satisfying rice cakes as a quick high-protein snack.

Peanut Butter Banana Protein Bites

Ingredients:

- 2 ripe bananas
- 1 cup rolled oats
- ½ cup peanut butter
- 2 tablespoons honey
- ¼ cup protein powder

Macronutrient Breakdown (per serving - 2 bites):

- Protein: 8g
- Fat: 6g
- Carbs: 20g

Instructions:

- Mash bananas in a bowl, add oats, peanut butter, honey, and protein powder. Mix well.
- Shape into bite-sized balls and place them on a lined tray.
- Refrigerate for at least 30 minutes before serving.

Hummus and Veggie Sticks

Ingredients:

- 1 cup hummus
- Assorted veggie sticks (carrots, cucumber, bell peppers)

Macronutrient Breakdown (per serving):

- Protein: 8g
- Fat: 10g
- Carbs: 20g

Instructions:

- Purchase pre-made hummus or make your own by blending chickpeas, tahini, olive oil, garlic, and lemon juice.
- Wash and cut veggies into sticks.
- Dip veggie sticks into hummus and enjoy.

Peanut Butter Banana Protein Smoothie

Ingredients:

- 2 ripe bananas
- 2 tablespoons peanut butter
- 1 cup almond milk
- 1 scoop protein powder

Macronutrient Breakdown (per serving):

- Protein: 20g
- Fat: 12g
- Carbs: 35g

Instructions:

- Blend ripe bananas, peanut butter, almond milk, and protein powder until smooth.
- Add more liquid if needed for desired consistency.
- Serve immediately.

References

1. Smith, J. (2020). Not a Diet Book: Take Control. Gain Confidence. Change your Life. HarperCollinsPublishers.

2. Popkin, B. M., D'Anci, K. E., & Rosenburg, I H. (2011). Water, Hydration and Health. Nutrition Reviews, 68(8), 439-458.

3. Carreiro, A. L., Dhillon, J., Gordon, S., Higgins, K. A., Jacobs, A. G., McArthur, B. M., Redan, B. W., Rivera, R. L., Schmidt, L. R., Mattes, R. D. (2016). The Macronutrients, Appetite, and Energy Intake. Annual Review of Nutrition, 17(36), 73-103.

4. Harris, J., & Benedict, F. (2020) A Biometric Study of Basal Metabolism in Man. Alpha Editions.

5. Mifflin, M. D., St Jeor, S. T., Hill, L. A., Scott, B., & Daugherty, S. A. (1990). A New Predictive Equation for Resting Energy Expenditure in Healthy Individuals. The American Journal of Clinical Nutrition, 51(2), 241-247.

6. Rodriguez, N. R., DiMarco, N. M., & Langley , S. (2009). Position of the American Dietetic Association, Dietitians of Canada, and the American Collage of Sports Medicine: Nutrition and Athletic Performance. Journal of the American Dietetic Association, 109(3), 509-527.

7. Wardlaw, G. M., & Smith, A. M. (2007). "Contemporary Nutrition." McGraw-Hill Higher Education.

8. Phillips, S. M. (2014). A brief review of critical processes in exercise-induced muscular hypertrophy. Sports Medicine, 44(1), 71-77.

9. Burke, L. M. (2015). Re-examining high-fat diets for sports performance: Did we call the 'nail in the coffin' too soon? Sports Medicine, 45(1), S33-S49.

10. Casa, D. J., et al. (2010). National Athletic Trainers' Association Position Statement: Fluid Replacement for Athletes. Journal of Athletic Training, 45(3), 385-389.

About the Author

Coach Nick Schofield

Nick is a military veteran with 24 years of military service. He started his health and fitness education back in 2007 completing his Personal Training and Sport massage course. Since then, he has completed numerous courses including a Degree in Sport Science and a master's degree in Strength and Conditioning.

Nick is a well-rounded professional with a passion for health and fitness. His experience in elite football, Exercise Rehabilitation Instruction, and Strength and Conditioning Coaching has given him a diverse set of skills and knowledge. Nick understands that nutrition is an essential aspect of overall wellness and has made it a priority to educate his patients and clients on the importance of a healthy diet. His background in functional food and sports nutrition has equipped him with the tools to provide valuable advice to those seeking to achieve their fitness and performance goals.

Nick's current focus is on supporting individuals who are joining the emergency services and military. He recognizes the physical demands that come with these careers and works diligently to prepare his clients for the rigors of service life. Additionally, Nick is pursuing a PhD in biomechanics to further his knowledge in injury management and identification.

Printed in Great Britain
by Amazon